KU-363-066

On the Evening Road

Dannie Abse

Hutchinson
London

© Dannie Abse 1994

The right of Dannie Abse to be identified as Author of this
work has been asserted by Dannie Abse in accordance with the
Copyright, Designs and Patents Act, 1988

All rights reserved

This edition first published in 1994 by Hutchinson

2 4 6 8 9 7 5 3 1

Random House (UK) Ltd
20 Vauxhall Bridge Road, London SW1V 2SA

Random House Australia (Pty) Ltd
20 Alfred Street, Milsons Point, Sydney, NSW 2061, Australia

Random House New Zealand Ltd
18 Poland Road, Glenfield, Auckland 10, New Zealand

Random House South Africa (Pty) Ltd
PO Box 337, Bergvlei, 2012, South Africa

A CiP catalogue record for this book is available from the
British Library

ISBN: 0 09 178941 9

Set in Bembo by SX Composing Ltd, Rayleigh, Essex
Printed and bound in Great Britain by
Mackays of Chatham plc, Chatham, Kent

NORFOLK LIBRARY AND INFORMATION SERVICE	
SUPPLIER	HJ
INVOICE No.	305083
ORDER DATE	8.9.94
COPY No.	

821 ABS

NOR:PA

Thanks are owed to the editors of the following journals in which a number of the poems in *On the Evening Road* first appeared: *Acumen, Aquarius, The Author, European Judaism, A Garland for Stephen Spender, Illuminations, The Jewish Quarterly, London Magazine, The New Statesman, The New Welsh Review, New Writing* (British Council), *The Observer, Pivot* (New York), *Ploughshares* (Boston), *The Poetry Book Society Anthology 2, Poetry* (Chicago), *Poetry Review, Poetry Wales, Quarterly Review of Literature* (Princeton), *The Spectator, The Sunday Times.*

Contents

Proposal

Herschel, thrilled, observed a new star
and named it to honour a King;

Dr Livingstone found for his Queen
a waterfall 'smoke which sounded';

and tactful Corot gave Daumier
a house 'to upset the landlord'.

What dare I promise? Mountain signposts
are few and treasures I have none.

Yet come with me, congenial, far,
up the higher indigo roads.

There, memory is imagination
and we may find an eagle's feather.

The Green Field

As soft-eyed lovers for the very first time,
turning out the light for the first time,
blot out all detail, all colours,
and whisper the old code-words, 'Love you',

so those admiring that patch of grass,
there, on the hillside, from this distance
could be in the dark, unconcerned with detail.
'That green field,' they generalise,

though drawing nearer (as to a poem)
they will discover the lies of distance:
rage of different greens. And at the field itself
an unforeseen tapestry of variousness:

sprawl of common weeds and wild flowers,
subtleties of small petals seldom green.

Talking to Blake

I saw a lit candle in sunlight
held by the ghost of William Blake.
He walked by the polluted river, ill-at-ease,
beneath Lambeth's dusty poplar trees.

Then high above Parliament Big Ben struck
and his voice advised as from afar,
'Write visionary lines that give a moral light,
let a poem become a star.'

'Mr Blake,' I replied, 'most poets make
a pale sound now – like a falling snowflake
and the roar of machinery grows
with the automation of the rose.

Deafened, deafened, are the beautiful Nine
so what you once said remains as true,
the languid strings do scarcely move,
the sound is forc'd, the notes are few.

All our permutations of despair,
smouldering word-fires without light or heat,
our pursuance of the incomplete,
leave no disturbance in the air.'

'Then,' said he, lowering the candlestick,
(as if to examine a grain of sand)
'the Rose of English Poetry is sick
like England's green and pleasant land.'

Condensation on a Windowpane

1

I want to write something simple,
something simple, few adjectives,
ambiguities disallowed.

Something old-fashioned:
a story of Time perhaps
or, more daringly, of love.

I want to write something simple
that everyone can understand,
something simple as pure water.

But pure water
is H_2O
and that's complicated
like steam, like ice, like clouds.

2

My finger squeaks on glass.
I write JOAN
I write DANNIE.
Imagine! I'm a love-struck
youth again.

I want to say something
without ambiguity.
Imagine! me, old-age pensioner
wants to say something
to do with love and Time,
love that's simple as water.

But long ago we learnt
water is complicated,
is H_2O, is ice, is steam, is cloud.

Our names on the window
begin to fade.
Slowly, slowly.
They weep as they vanish.

How I won the Raffle

After I won the raffle with the number 1079,
the Master of Ceremonies asked me why.
'Why did you select that particular number?'

'A man's character is his fate,' I replied,
leaning lazily on a quote as usual.

And suddenly I thought of Schopenhauer's
two last men in the world, two gaunt hermits,
meeting each other in the wilderness,

how an amiable man like Pufendorf
might postulate they'd shake hands;
a Hobbes they'd kill each other;
a Rousseau they'd pass each other by
in terrible silence.

'In short,' said the Master of Ceremonies impatiently,
'you chose 1079 because you had to.'

'In short, I chose 10 because in the old days
ten men used to dance around a new grave.

I chose 7 because those ten men used to dance
around the new grave seven times.'

Also because of the pyramids of Egypt;
the hanging gardens of Babylon;
Diana's Temple at Ephesus;
the great statue of Zeus at Athens;
the Mausoleum at Halicarnassus;
the Colossus of Rhodes;
and the lighthouse of Alexandria.

'I chose 9 because among all numbers
it looks most like a musical note;
nine because of the nine orders of Angels;
nine because of the nine rivers of Hell.'

Also because of Clio with her backward look;
Calliope, stern, staring at her scroll;
Erato, nude, except for her brassière;
Euterpe, eyes closed, flute in mouth;
Terpsichore dancing away, silly one;
Melpomene, arms raised, dagger in hand;
Thalia, mirthless, behind her laughing mask;
Polyhymnia, in sacred robes, orating;
and Urania, dreamy, head amid the stars.

'Sir,' I said,
to the scowling Master of Ceremonies,
'that's why I chose the winning number
1079.'

Between 3 and 4 a.m.

1

Wakeful at 3 a.m.
near the frontiers of Nothing
it's easy, so easy
to imagine (like William Blake)
an archaic angel standing
in a cone of light
not of this world;

easy at the cheating hour
to believe an angel cometh
to touch babies' skulls,
their fontanelles,
deleting the long memory
of generations –
(only prodigies not visited);

easy to conceive angel-light
bright as that sudden,
ordinary window
I saw at midnight
across the road
before the drawing
of its blind.

2

Once, another presence
also nocturnal, oneiric,
secretive, in disguise,
waiting behind
an opening Seder door.

'No,' says the child. 'Gone.'
Framed in that black oblong,
nobody.

(A shadow flies
when a light is shone.)

Was childhood real?
Did a stallion attempt
to mount a mare
painted by Apelles?
Did Greek workmen hear
the exiled statue sob
when carried to
Lord Elgin's ship?

The mystery named
is not the mystery caged.

Even a night-scene
may be an illusion
like an afternoon harbour
viewed through sunglasses,
the light forged
to a moon-tortured sea.

3

I was visited once, once only, elsewhere,
near a lake, near an oak,
near a weeping willow tree and thorn
one summertime, out of time, in England,
during the cosmic love-making hour
when day and night shyly intermingled,
when day, entranced, did not know what or who
and night, ecstatic, was not itself entirely

till the slow coming of the stars.

But now, weeping willow tree and thorn,
there's only the dread of Nothing.

(Nothing, say the kabbalists
is more real than nothing.)

It's 4 a.m. already and cold
and quiet, quiet as a long
abandoned battlefield.

Late to trawl, net full of holes,
the grounded darkness
for what, naturally, can never be told.

(The unutterable, at best, becomes music.)

No, it's time to hold the silence found
on one side
with the right hand,
the silence on the other
with the left,
then to pull, pull, pull,

till silence tears without a sound.

The Mistake

Come this way through the wooden gate into our
    garden.
Confront the green tree which once had no identity.
Pluck a leaf. Close your eyes. Smell its acrid odour.
Does it suggest an Oriental dispensary?

One day (after thirteen years) a tree-expert told us
its name: '*Evodia danieli*, without doubt.
From Korea. Odd to find it thriving here in Wales.'
We thanked him. Now we had something to boast
    about.

When visitors came we offered them a leaf proudly.
'Breathe this in,' we'd urge. 'It's rare as Welsh gold.'
Our olfactory gift, our pagan benediction.
'From Korea,' we'd swank. 'It'll charm away your
    cold.'

Who, in all of Great Britain, possessed such treasure?
But then came the summer of the drought. Tired of
    lies
the parched tree suddenly asserted itself, sprouted
ordinary walnuts, shamelessly free of disguise.

A Doctor's Register

And yet God has not said a word!
                              Porphyria's Lover, *R. Browning*

Half asleep, you recalled a fading list
of girls' sweet names. Now to old women
these names belong – some whom you tumbled and
    kissed
in summer's twilit lanes or hidden by heather.
You were a youth who never stayed long
for Gwen or for Joyce, for Rita or Ruth
and there were others too, on a lower register.

Then, suddenly, a robust, scolding voice
changed your dream's direction and the weather:
'That much morphia, doctor? Wrong, wrong.'

Surprised to discover your eyes still shut
you wondered which dead patient or what
(whose accusing son and when?) as any
trusted doctor would who did not murder
any pleading one with sovereign impunity.

'I found a thing to do,' said the lover
of Porphyria. *Porphyria?* Awake you add
the other pretty names too: Anuria,
Filaria, Leukaemia, Melanoma,
Sarcoma, Euthanasia, amen.

The Excavation

Absurd those tall stories of tall heroes.
Mine, too. Sixty ells, they said, between
my shoulders! Happy legends of my strength!
Hippy myths of my hair! How I lifted up
a mountain here, a mountain there. Dig, dig:
so little recorded, so many exaggerations.

Three hundred foxes, they said, remember?
Nine, only nine. With a jawbone of an ass,
they said, I topped a thousand men. Dig, dig
for their gritty skulls. I unthatched a mere ten.
Let others boast that I was 'magic',
the rainbow spirit of the Lord about me.

But absent, He, when the whips cracked and I
was led, eyeless, into Dagon's Temple,
heard the hooting crazies on the roof. So many,
the junk Temple collapsed thunderously.
Joke! They thought *I'd* brought the House down –
me, clapped-out circus act, defunct Strong Man.

I was screaming, believe me, I was lost.
Betrayed, betrayed, and so little recorded:
the brevities of a Hebrew scribe only;
a fable for a Milton to embroider;
a picture for a Rubens to paint;
music for the soul of a Saint-Saëns.

Dig, dig, though you will not find Dagon's stone
fish-tail nor the scissors of the sung star
of the Philistines. Who knows the path of that whore
after the Temple, unglued, crashed and crushed?
Did she return to Sorek or raise once more
her aprons in the brothels of Philistia?

Dig, dig. I hear your questing spades muffled,
south of Gaza. Useless. The shifting sands
have buried deeper the graves of all.
Only the wilderness remains, silence
and a jawbone. And marvellous ghosts
people a yellow page of Judges.

History

(To Peter Vansittart)

The last war-horse slaughtered and eaten
long ago. Not a rat, not a crow-crumb
left; the polluted water scarce;
the vile flies settling on the famous
enlarged eyes of skeleton children.

Tonight the moon's open-mouthed. I must
surrender in the morning. But those
cipher tribes out there, those Golden Hordes,
those shit! They'll loot and maim and rape.
What textbook atrocities in the morning?

Now, solitary, my hip-joint aching,
half-lame, I climb the high battlements
carrying a musical instrument.
Why not? What's better? The bedlam of sleep
or the clarities of insomnia?

Look! Below, most fearful perspective:
cloud-fleeing shadows of unending
flatlands; enemy tent after tent
pegged to the unstable moonlight.
You'd think the moon, exposed, would howl.

Besieged city, in some future
history book (aseptic page or footnote)
they'll fable your finale: how
your huck-shouldered, arthritic General,
silhouette on the dark battlements,

played on his pipe a Mongolian song,
an enemy song, played so purely
the Past disrobed, memory made audible,
(sharp as a blade, lonely, most consequent,
that soul-naked melody of the steppes);

how, below, the Mongol soldiers awoke,
listened, leaned on their elbows tamed,
became so utterly homesick, wretched,
so inflamed, that by the cold sweats
of dawnlight, they decamped, departed.

Ha! Such a pleasing, shameless story,
to be told over and over by these
and by those: by propagandists of music;
by descendants of the Mongols.
But, alas, only a scribe's invention.

The truth? I play pianissimo
and not very well. The sleepers
in their tents sleep on, the sentries
hardly stir. I loiter on the battlements.
Stars! Stars! I put away my pipe and weep.

Meurig Dafydd to his Mistress

No word I huffed when Stradling urged the squire
to throw my eulogy on the fire.
The fiddlers laughed. I, snow-silent, proud,
did not melt. But I'm spitless now,
my pearl, my buttercup, my bread-fruit.
I rattle their silver in my pocket.
I have other stanzas for harp and lute,
other gullible lords to flatter.
What do I care for that big-bellied Englishman,
that bugle, that small-beer, that puff-ball,
that dung-odoured sonneteer, John Stradling?

Does he sing perfect metre like Taliesin?
Not that gout-toed, goat-faced manikin.
What does he know of Welsh necks crayoned
by the axe, blood on our feet, our history?
Has he stood pensive at the tomb
of Morien, or Morial, or March?
Wept at any nervous harp, at the gloom
of a dirge for Llywelyn the Last,
or the lament by Lewis Glyn Cothi?
That fungoid, that bunt, that broken-wind,
that bog-bean, can't tell a song from a grunt.

Clean heart, my theology, my sweet-briar,
he'd put our heritage on the fire.
Each night he swigs mead in a safe bed –
never sleeps roofed only by the stars.
At noon, never signs the euphonious nine
sermons of the blackbird. O my lotus,
his lexicon is small compared to mine.

His verses are like standing urine – tepid.
My Welsh stanzas have more heat in them
than the tumbling flames in the fire-place
of the Minstrel Hall of Bewpyr.

Ya

The machine began to hum.
Some blood, they pleaded,
just a little, uncoagulated,
fresh blood, please.
It was springtime, springtime,
the season to open doors.
A pinprick? On the thumb?
They shook their heads.
Hesitant, scrupulous,
sullenly, we detached a finger
– under an anaesthetic,
humanely, you understand.
But, afterwards, candid,
they demanded, More blood!
And, ya, after debate
we did amputate a hand:
soft tissues retracted,
joint opened cleanly,
lateral ligaments cut through.
From the wrist.
Better, they said hoarsely,
leaving us discomfited.
What else could we do?
Outside it was springtime, springtime,
the birds' hullabaloo;
the young cried as usual,
not knowing why,
the old because they knew.
So, ya, a whole arm,
almost a perfect job
and without an anaesthetic too.

18

No wonder they applauded,
their obscene shouts, their keen whistles,
like hosannas from hell.
Allow us this though;
outside it was shifting sunlight,
it was wild bluebells
and, ya, one of us at the window
quoted an English poet-priest:
I do not think I've seen
anything more beautiful
than a bluebell.
I know the beauty
of our Lord by it.
So not till all the women
were released, banished,
did we consent to saw off
a raw foot. Right and left neatly,
our technique swift, improving.
And who could not respond
excitedly – that adrenal flow –
to their rhythmic chanting?
Ya, with both legs wide
then unhinged completely,
oh the powerful voltage
of their male applause
and oh the soulful thrilling
of our National Anthem.
So moving, so very moving,
man it was something.
Fellow scientists,
you can guess
what happened next,
ya, you know
the end of the story.

Beautiful Dead Poets

She spoke of Garcia Lorca murdered;
Hernandez dying in a Franco prison;
Mayakovsky's suicide; how Mandelstam
jumped through the window of a hospital;
Celan and Levi in the Nazi Death Camps.
'Beautiful dead poets, all of them,' said she,
in the delight of enthusiasm.

Behind her, a dark mahogany table
that once had the girth of a lofty tree;
a vase of deep red, drooping lovely things –
aged tulips – untimely ripped from the earth;
and, by the window, a canary caged
because it sang so beautifully.

Ghosting for Mayakovsky

(His suicide note)

1

It's long past one and you must be asleep.
The quiet night's astonished by all the stars.
Why wake you now with a telegram like thunder?

So many thoughts of mystery the night can bring.
So what? Our love boat's on the rocks. Its sails
wrenched from the mast. No use in adding up the
   cost,

we're quits; no need to weigh our hearts and hurts
upon the scales. 'No Life without you,' once I said,
and now the strokes of Two thud down like heads
   from blocks.

Our story's over, iconoclast. I'm lost. I'm through.
No need to wake you with a telegram like thunder.
Art's imperative will make these lines come true.

2

Once I drew the Queen of Hearts,
now I'm dealt another card. A club. A two.
Once forbidden love lit up like paper
then it charred.

Once with verse of lightning and half in song
I told a daisy and the world
you loved me, you love me not,
and how worthless life unfurled would be
without you – like a single shoe.
I'll not limp along.

I'm shot. I'm through.
Queen of Hearts, O Queen of Hearts,
the imperatives of Art insist,
the lies of Art come true.

Is Creation a Destructive Force?

1

Weary in the airport lounge
he read again the letters of Keats:
'I am with Achilles in the trenches,
with Theocritus in the vales of Sicily.'

Later, at the airport security,
crossing the doorless door,
an empty, revolver-like
click–terrorist, click–terrorist, click.

They searched him,
checked his identification papers,
found in his inside pocket
the pen that can annihilate self.

2

In the studio where she suddenly died,
on the easel still, Ingeborg's last canvas,
entrancing, unfinished, and of course unsigned.

Afflicted self-portrait. She crouches before
a half-open door – there's dark darkness behind
and, just visible, a stark foot's advancing.

Ludic Oblongs

First draw an oblong on an unlined page,
the shape of the page. Now what do you see?

No, Peter, no. Not an upright coffin.
Hardly, it's much too wide for a coffin.

A magician's box. Uh huh. Suppose so.
From which the blonde lady has disappeared

no doubt. What do you think, Melanie? Yes.
A window. Right. What do you see through it?

Snowfields? Acres of snowfields on and on?
Quiet, Mary. It's Melanie's window.

What? A frosted window? C'mon, hardly.
Someone in a bath behind it, perhaps?

Why are you laughing, Peter? What's that, Paul?
Mmm. A cage without bars. The bird has flown.

The bell rang then and I went home happy
till I thought of the real world and its ills.

Oh the uselessness of drawing oblongs
filled with trapped silence or white on white.

Still, here's another, here's its caption:
THE LOST WALK IN THE SAME DIRECTION

Breakfast Together

She sits opposite me
the other side of the breakfast table,
doesn't know that last week
I murdered her.

Oh pure, flawless love!
It would have altered – leaves are falling now –
with the passing years.

Consider the statistics of divorce.
The possible prolegomenon:
secret phone-calls,
furtive appointments,
marital violence even.

Man, man, never strike a woman
for if you do
she'll have dominion
over you.

No, no, not that. None of that
as the leaves fall, the passing years.

So I arranged her funeral,
no expense spared –
a secular funeral; a hush of black cars;
flowers galore, a veritable park!

The mortician's arms folded, head bowed.

I thought of playing that tape,
that Beethoven *Cavatina*,
that anguished music she loved best,
music so remote, so terrible.

Instead I chose the old dance-tune
my mother-in-law liked:
'Stay as sweet as you are,
don't let a thing ever change you.'
Appropriate, *n'est-ce-pas?*

Afterwards, the wake that I had planned.
A joyous feast! Drinks galore!
We had everything except balloons.

And there she is now, not knowing any of this,
sitting the other side of the table,
alluring still, spooning a grapefruit,
mirthless, reading the *Guardian* –
she, only one week less perfect.

Chocolate Box

Late neglected November, Leporello,
and more back-garden rosy-red apples
decorated the tree than countable leaves
when she, through the window,
saw a blue-tit on a bough.

Sighed: 'What an unbelievable pretty picture,
an old-fashioned chocolate box.'

Later, surprised, thinking of unpicked apples,
of course I tasted her red pretty mouth.

Later still, at twilight, the unwrapping.
Her falling black dress rustling
like chocolate-paper;

and the whole delicious
old-fashioned, Rubens-beautiful
box open. Offered and taken: truffle,
cherry liqueur, marzipan, Turkish Delight.

Legacy

Savages adore personal ornament
so take my rose-cut diamond made of glass,
 my brass diadem, my false pearls.

Take my brooch that tries to look like amber,
the earrings you covet, my brummagems.
 Alas, few loaves, fewer fish.

Darling, for you my only brilliants.
For you, my best, my sapphire-like marbles
 plundered from a child's tin box.

My fake gold bangle you may also keep,
that which I won with a wooden ball
 at an Easter fair in Ponty.

I bequeath too my paste-jewel husband.
Bed that bad trickster as you've longed to do –
 my woolworth man, my worthless drag.

Lastly, darling, wear my slave's iron ring.
You'll find beneath its secret bezel
 poison for an emergency.

Divorce Proceedings

(Harriet's)

Am I, this April, an April Fool?
I'll not accept your handshake-offer:
'Friendship' – though what persists of love
lies chilled in the past, illusory,
like the far, voyaging light of a star.

I'm not benign like Shelley's Harriet, no,
though pregnant as she was and as wretched.
I'll not saccharine a suicide-note,
'Dear one, God bless and watch over you,'
then grow hideous in the Serpentine.

Or be helpless like pill-taking Sylvia,
incandescent with desperation,
those oneiric poems like sos's,
before full-stopping the riderless heart
with the head, eyes open, in the oven.

Yet once, like her, I hoped for a hundred-
piece orchestra, and Brahms and Mahler,
not a thin dance-tune on a comb;
a happy-ever-after golden crown,
not a dunce's paper hat, twee and tatty.

Don't you see? It's the corybantic poetry
of love's adult passion I long for still,
its wild rhyming and its cadences
– this the dismayed heart of it – not
the attenuated prose of friendship,

your mild pity. God rot your smiling teeth.
The pretty blossom's looted, betrayed,
the wind and the cold of it – April's
practical joke: the trees' confetti
wet and finished in the gutters.

Evergreens

1

'Death? That's for other people,'
Billy Lucas used to say,
sad, sunny-side up, verbal Billy Lucas.

It's winter now in his closed shop-doorway.

He used to roll up his trousers,
dart towards an autumn tree
quicker than a dog-hunted cat
and, at the quivering top, shout out
with spotless joy, 'I am immortal!'

Sometimes he seemed to be
the happiest patient
in that hospital of sorrows.

It's winter now in the grounds of St Ebbas.

The tall deciduous trees have staged
their own phoney funerals
(such morbid, such colourful rehearsals)
and pose for black and white photography.

Who'll cry, 'Long live manic denial,'
esteem the cedar and the yew
and all euphoric Evergreens?

2

It's summer now in the Municipal Gardens.
I know a consoling fountain there. Sssh, surprise:
a cherub, copper greenish-blue, juggles
4 open-mouthed, water-spouting fish. Look! one
  more
peeing trout has landed between his thighs.

I pass a hoarse-voiced, overbearded crazy
on a wooden bench. It seems that he prays
to this small fat idol who juggles behind
sunlit shatterings of water. The cherub, of course,
smiles on – insouciant and ecstatic and blind.

Shmelke

(For A.B.)

Consider the chassidic story of Shmelke
the wise, the celebrated Shmelke of Nikolsburg:
how he, to be honoured among men,
to be word-oiled and garlanded
at the ceremony of ten
dozen uplifted beards,
demanded, first, a room with a mirror.

Before it he stood, head to toe,
solemnly cooing, 'Lo, you are wonderful, Shmelke,
you are generous and compassionate;
you are an eagle above the stars;
you take root downward, bear fruit upward;
you have the energy of broad rivers;
you leap like a hart over the green herb,
over the grass in the field. You are deft,
seemly, and beautiful of countenance.
Shmelke, you are a paragon of virtue;
you are peerless, flawless, humorous,
spiritual like the orange blossom.
You are a saint, Shmelke, holy, holy, holy,
the earth a mere syllable of your glory.'

Those near the portals observing Shmelke,
overhearing Shmelke, were puzzled, disturbed.

'But I was merely preparing myself
by uttering absurdities to the mirror,'
said Shmelke. 'Now I'm ready for your compliments.
Lead me to the platform, let us proceed.'

Cricket Ball

1935, I watched Glamorgan play
especially Slogger Smart, free
from the disgrace of fame, unrenowned,
but the biggest hit with me.

A three-spring flash of willow
and suddenly, the sound of summer
as the thumped ball, alive, would leave
the applauding ground.

Once, hell for leather, it curled
over the workman's crane
in Westgate Street
to crash, they said, through a discreet
Angel Hotel windowpane.

But I, a pre-war boy,
(or someone with my name)
wanted it, that Eden day,
to scoot around the turning world,
to mock physics and gravity,
to rainbow-arch the posh hotel
higher, deranged, on and on, allegro,
(the Taff a gleam of mercury below)
going, going, gone
towards the Caerphilly mountain range.

Vanishings! The years, too, gone like change.
But the travelling Taff seems the same.
It's late. I peer at the failing sky
over Westgate Street
and wait. I smell cut grass.
I shine an apple on my thigh.

Two Photographs

Here's a photograph of grandmother, Annabella.
How slim she appears, how vulnerable. Pretty.
And here's a photograph of grandmother, Doris.
How portly she looks, formidable. Handsome.
Annabella wears a demure black frock with an amber
  brooch.
Doris, a lacy black gown with a string of pearls.
One photo's marked *Ystalyfera* 1880,
the other *Bridgend* 1890.
Both were told to say, 'Cheese'; one, defiant, said 'Chalk!'

Annabella spoke Welsh with a Patagonian accent.
Doris spoke English with a Welsh Valleys' lilt.
Annabella fasted – pious, passive, enjoyed small-talk.
Doris feasted – pacy, pushy, would never pray. Ate pork!
When Annabella told Doris she was damned
indecorous Doris devilishly laughed.
I liked Doris, I liked Annabella,
though Doris was bossy and Annabella daft.
I do not think they liked each other.

Last night I dreamed they stood back to back,
not for the commencement of a duel
but to see who was taller! Now, in these revived
waking hours, my Eau de Cologne grandmothers
with buns of grey hair, of withered rose,
seem illusory, fugitive, like my dream –
or like the dust that secretively flows
in a sudden sunbeam (sieved through leaky curtains)
and disappears when and where that sunbeam goes.

Of two old ladies once uxoriously loved,
what's survived? An amber brooch, a string of pearls,
two photographs. Happening on them, my children's
grandchildren will ask 'Who?' – hardly aware
that if this be not true, I never lived.

In the National Gallery

Each single angel is terrible
                    R. M. Rilke

Not these, hardly these, not even Piero's
smoothy-faced St Michael, despite big sword
in one hand, nasty snake's head in other;
certainly not the angel Gabriel, mild,
bored with his pose of kneeling and caught again
in the flashlight eyes of wild Fra Lippi:

all said and done, a mere silly, pre-pubertal boy
with a simpering look of 'Gee, you're pregnant!',
overdressed in Sunday-best, peacock's wings
that would not lift him higher than a tree.
And those other angels (God permitting)
who granted impure painters with pure ability

a sitting – how unhappy they appear,
androgynous, holy ones with male names
(designated legends ago, of course, by men)
so tame, surely, that if you cried hosannas,
clapped hands loudly, they'd disappear slowly
back to vast Invisibility.

But that stranger there, so corporeal,
who scowls now at the sweet Virgin of the Rocks,
is he, perhaps, in disguise even to himself,
a descendant of Azazel or Shemhazai?
And others who come in from Trafalgar Square
to be fazed by the fangless spell of moral Art

are they secretly terrible – offspring
of fallen angels and daughters of men:
hair-raising Emim whose glance can stop the heart;
Zamzummim, masters and monsters in war;
Nephilim, called such, since they brought this world
to its still falling fall when they themselves fell?

In the Villa Borghese

The chase. Through the wood, the terror of it.
The choice. Violent love or vegetable asylum.
Still true, sometimes, for uncertain men.
Still true, sometimes, for certain women.
She, with the soul of a nun, chose.

In the Villa Borghese they have become marble.
Millions of days, millions of nights
they pose. He, too, ironically petrified.

With a stethoscope I want to hear
their two hearts beat within the marble.
I want to put a mirror to their mouths.

According to Ovid, she chose. Who cried?
She left him priapic and aching.
Did it rain then? Did he lift his god's leg?

Now I hear, outside, the seminal patter of it
on wide laurel leaves. No matter,
a tree might welcome such fresh drenching.

A feminist victory? Hardly.
True, one more heavy breather denied –
unless, of course, Ovid, pleasing some prim,
some god-loving, soma-loathing priest,
sweetened an older, raunchier story. Lied.

Destinies

(To Francis Celoria)

Sometimes the gods appear to be insane.
So addicted to metamorphosis!
Pity the unloved vulture flying above a roof,
pity the lone eagle settling on a mountain.

Long ago, 'Hail Periphas!' cried the populace
and built a great temple in his honour;
began to call him, 'Overlooker of All'
and at the agora, 'Your Imperial Grace',

offending big-jawed Zeus. His boss-face gorged
with anger – he, flash lord of the thunderbolts,
scandalous incinerator of men –
bridled his ten white horses and charged

over boiling plains toward the Aegean shore
where that afternoon, in sand-dune amour,
Periphas, anastomosing with Phene, sighed,
'Dear one,' while she replied, 'Love evermore!'

Four times unignorable Zeus tapped
the busy bare back of rapt Periphas.
Alas, when Periphas turned he was turned
into a bird, into an eagle that flapped

its wings till Phene, flushed, opened her eyes.
First, surprise. Then appalling cries were heard;
but still she, faithful wife, begged to become
bird also. 'Please Judicious One, All-wise.'

Praised, the god, red-toothed, smiled. Would he
    concur?
Her nakedness fled and she was covered
with feathers till, heart and head, Phene was
all bird, all sorry-looking vulture.

The sweetness of feminine self-denial!
Are male saints, unmasked, deceiving women?
Other men become wolves to savage other men
so who'd arraign Zeus? Put the gods on trial?

They pester with vipers the sleep of mankind
and, like men, won't forgive those they've injured.
What horrors have they in mind, what
    transformations
in the zoo of Time to come? To prove unkind?

Sometimes the gods cannot remain aloof
when the populace love a man too much.
Pity the lone eagle flying about a mountain.
Pity the unloved vulture settling on a roof.

Just One of Those Days, William

Back from your id-holiday in Greece,
closing the front door behind you,
oh unlikely omen, your left foot stepped
on the silence of an ant. Deleted!
Just one of those days, William.

Soon after, you passed the Reservoir,
saw a crow flying with seagulls,
taking off when they did, trying
to alight when they did, desperate
to float on water – defeated.

Then, at the office, the Three appeared.
You were bugged. They knew your liaison
with Lais. Demanded drachmas,
and clicked their castrating scissors.
Just one of those days, William,

like that when naughty Icarus,
ignoring his father's advice
(the old taboo), dared illicit elevation –
wild on a high, happy as vice,
till he felt both wings shift, unglue;

like that when cissy Narcissus
espied a pretty boy in the pool
(the insolence of imitation!).
The fool drowned trying to embrace him.
Just one of those days, William.

Lunchtime, unmerry in 'The Bear',
you waited hours for the waiters,
Agrius and Orius. Each weighed a ton.
They sat in the cockroached kitchen,
big teeth chewing more than a bun.

Back at the office, you found faeces on
the Turkish carpet, drawers flung open,
phone wires cut, oak desk smashed,
and, uninsured, the Golden Fleece gone.
Just one of those days, William,

like that when Zeus descended – uncouth,
hauled Periphas off nude Phene,
then turned those lovers into birds:
he, an eagle to the mountain,
she, a vulture to the roof;

like that when bare–chested Hylas
while rowing across the river
was dragged below the water
by nymphomaniacal nymphs.
Just one of those days, William.

And they talk of Sod's malicious law,
the wincing unease of not knowing
what you have long forgotten,
and that as you are to an ant
someone, Someone, may be to you.

Touch Wood

Come, let us praise wood
no longer agrestial.
Not the trillions of coffins
but wood within a living house,
the quietude of an empty bookcase,
the loneliness of scattered chairs –
the metamorphosis
of trees, shrubs, bushes, twigs.
Doors particularly, upstairs, downstairs,
whatever their disposition,
welcoming, half open,
or secretively shut.

It does not matter.
Delightful the craftsmanship
of their lintels,
so comely, so pleasant,
like the repeated oblongs
of windowframes, upstairs, downstairs,
like the serenity of windowsills
that carry vases, flower-pots.
And who could not respond
to the utilitarian elegance
of a wide staircase
rising from a parquet floor?

What a history wood has,
what old echoing stories
in the random museum of the mind:
the gopher ark of Noah
floating high above the mountains;
the huge, staring Trojan horse;

Diogenes's fat barrel;
Horatius's one-way bridge
that fell into the Tiber;
King Arthur's Round Table –
all these relics lost forever
like Jesus's insensate Cross.

Sometimes I think we should construct
in the garden of a living house
an idol of various woods:
head of Lombardy Poplar,
trunk of reliable Oak,
arms of Elm and Pine,
hands of Lime and Plane,
legs of Birch and Beech,
feet of grainy Sycamore
and genitals (of course, discreet)
of musty Fig tree, untidy Fir
and the droopy Weeping Willow.

November nights when we're asleep,
when unbuttoned winds shake the house,
what the spirit of the house
if not the spirit of the forest?
What replies if not primal wood,
dryad-ghost and Daphne-creak,
wild cries of wood awakening?
We, stern-faced as mourners, slumber on,
carry in dream the golden bough
from some black forgotten tree
of the windless underworld
back to the leaf-strewn morning.

Blessings and Curses

1 *Sunflowers*

I

Near the back-garden's West wall,
near a synagogue shemozzle of wasps
about michaelmas daisies,
a watchful congregation
of sunflowers in their Sunday best.

Guests of autumn, they too
are enslaved by religion.
Not Jewish or Moslem flowers these:
they pray to the sun,
turn to the South. Obsessed.

II

They do not hear her footsteps.
Choosing, she cuts twelve tall stems.
Held close, the green leaves curl
to the curve of her breast.

Chosen, no apostles these.
Stripped of their leaves, half undressed,
stiff with hubris, their anther-buttons
seem more blatantly manifest.
Twelve glorious atheists
free of the sun's power,
the tyranny of the sun.

The full vase an inflorescence of yellow,
an unashamed zest of yellow,
a musical purity of yellow,
and merely by admiring we are blessed.

47

2 *November Bonfire*

After the sunset ignited windows
then faded, the sky-dangle of fireworks.
Rockets whoosh towards haughty stars
from our acrid back-garden.
Each year the funeral pomp of autumn,
and soon we blaze up a log-fire
to incinerate a scarecrow.
Welcome, you pilgrims of light.
Sing, everybody, sing. Sing louder.
Why follow the arrow
of the huge blind archer?
Sing dirges for mortuary golden rods,
orisons for cadavers of sunflowers,
and higher and higher the log-fire.
Where else did the sunset go?

Now the children dance around it,
small corybants around it,
the singing and singing louder,
prancing dwarf shadows around it
to ward off inquisitive demons.
Light of the unlocked flames,
crack of the sparks flying,
heat of the timbers' alkalines.
Look! Listen! Feel! Sing! Dance!
The scarecrow's burning alive,
opening its mouth but once;
then, into ash, it collapses.

Hallelujah! Hallelujah! –
till all smell of wood-smoke,
till all, touch wood, be blessed.

3 Solace

On her deathbed my spunky mother
wishing to be left alone, not helped,
cursed me. My hand, mid-air, still as stone.
Her sudden gritty voice jarring and unjust,
a snarling stranger's voice, sister of one
who knew the 32 curses of Leviticus.
The Dukes of Edom would have been amazed,
the Mighty of Moab would have been undone.

That night each man cursed became my brother.

Today I read how Rabbi Simeon's son
had been vilely cursed: *May your permanent
home be ruined, may your temporary
abodes be built up*. 'These are blessings not
curses,' Simeon interpreted, cocksure.
'You are wished Long Life so that your own plot
in the family cemetery be ruined,
and the houses wherein you live endure.'

Sunday Night, Monday Morning

Not like the vandal wind outside
upturning trees, wooden park-seats.
Call me subtle, a click half-heard
opening or closing interior doors.

Upstairs, you open both your eyes,
sit up in bed, listening. Only a show
of moon-shadows, vague. Your head sinks
on a sinking pillow. Goodbye clock.

Your sleeping mind has timeless caves
where extinct creatures snore and stir.
I'm home there, like a troglodyte.
I'll find a Cuvier bone for you.

I'll paint dawn murals, you shall dream them.
(Asleep, how much does your breathing weigh?
The air above the clouds is heavier.)
Erotic one, throw high your silver stick.

Ho! A procession: unicorns (how chic),
tall soothsayers, red-gowned Chaldeans
with golden chains about their necks.
They follow you to morning's abattoir.

You draw the curtains back, I'm still here,
your aide-mémoire, your compass-needle,
your master that some call revenant
(quiet as the spider in the bath).

By what I am, know what you do.
You turn tap steam on, exit spider,
(some apocalypse, some aubade)
you wipe the mirror clear of dream.

Thankyou Note

for the unbidden swish of morning curtains
you opened wide – letting sleep-baiting shafts
of sunlight enter to lie down by my side;
for adagio afternoons when you did the punting
(my toiling eyes researched the shifting miles of sky);
for back-garden evenings when you chopped the
    wood
and I, incomparably, did the grunting;
(a man too good for this world of snarling
is no good for his wife – truth's the safest lie);

for applauding my poetry, O most perceptive spouse;
for the improbable and lunatic, my darling;
for amorous amnesties after rancorous rows
like the sweet-nothing whisperings of a leafy park
after the blatant noise of a city street
(exit booming cannons, enter peaceful ploughs);
for kindnesses the blind side of my night-moods;
for lamps you brought in to devour the dark.

On the Evening Road

A disgrace a man of my age
to have come this far and not to know;
the fields inert with ignorant mist,
the road between, lost, unsignposted.

I may as well sing a little
since no-one's around to hear me,
'The Song of Omega' my father sang
though the words I've mostly forgotten.

I may as well dance a bit, too,
since no-one's around to scold me:
'Disgrace, a man of his age singing
drunkenly – not knowing where he is.'

Now the Caladrius bird lands
as it must, on the road ahead of me
and drops its dung. Turn towards me, bird,
O turn, turn, with your yellow beak.

Notes

'History'

According to legend, a Chinese general defending a city long besieged by the Mongols climbed, late at night, on the battlements, knowing that in the morning he would have to surrender to the enemy encamped below. With utter sadness he played on his pipe a Mongolian melody. Such was the power of his music the Mongols became homesick and by dawn departed!

'Meurig Dafydd to his Mistress'

The ruins of Beaupre (in Welsh Bewpyr), a once magnificent Tudor mansion, can be visited in the Vale of Glamorgan. There, after Christmas in 1603, a party was held at which a local bard, Meurig Dafydd, declaimed his praise-poem dedicated to the squire. Afterwards Meurig was asked if he had another copy of his poem. 'No by my fayth,' replied the bard, 'but I hope to take a copie of that which I delivered to you.' John Stradling, one of the guests, an English man of letters, reported how the bard's praise-poem was then delivered to the fire. A version of this incident is related in *The Taliesin Tradition* by Emyr Humphreys (Seren Books, 1989).

'Ghosting for Mayakovsky'

On the morning of 14 April 1930, the Soviet poet, Mayakovsky, shot himself. A fragment from an unfinished longer poem was included in his suicide note. A memorable version of this fragment, translated by Erik Korn, can be found in *Modern European Verse* (Vista Books, 1964). I have impudently 'ghosted' a later imagined draft of Mayakovsky's unfinished suicide poem, leaning on a few lines of Korn's translation.

'Breakfast Together'

The origin of this poem may be found in *Forbidden Games and Video Poems*, the poetry of Yang Mu and Lo Ch'ing (University of Washington Press, 1993). See Lo Ch'ing's 'Self-Sacrifice'.

'Just One of Those Days, William'

In the Introduction to *The Metamorphosis of Antoninus Liberalis* (Routledge, 1992) Francis Celoria relates how a crow was observed imitating the movements of seagulls at Middlesex Reservoir, 'despite an obvious inability to cope with a watery element'.

Lais was a celebrated whore of Corinth visited by princes, noblemen, orators and philosophers.

Agrius and Orius were the huge offspring of
Polyphonte who had coupled with a bear.

Hylas was a river of Mysia where Hylas was
drowned. Francis Celoria has written that Hylas was
'a lone waif, young and too pretty for his own good'.

'On the Evening Road'

The Caladrius bird was a white prophetic bird of
medieval legend, supposed to visit the sick. If it
looked at the patient, he or she would recover; if the
bird looked away instead, the patient would die.

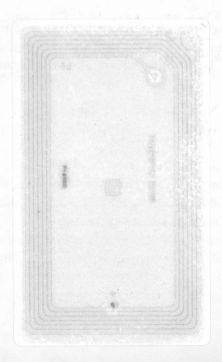